"I HAVE 12 KIDS…I HAVE TO CLOSE LOANS!"

MI-1632279 | Edge Home Finance Corporation supports Equal Housing Opportunity.
NMLS ID# 891464 (www.nmlsconsumeraccess.org). Interest rates and products are subject to change without notice and may or may not be available at the time of loan commitment or lock-in. Borrowers must qualify at closing for all benefits. This is not an offer to lend and each borrower must qualify on their own merit to purchase a home.

LEGAL NOTICE

DEDICATION

To my beautiful bride, Melissa "Bo"! Who has walked beside me since we were just a couple of high school kids with big dreams. You've been my anchor, my encourager, my home and you are "my person". Through every high and low, especially the valleys we never saw coming, your faith and fierce love never wavered. This wouldn't exist without you.

To our twelve amazing children and our growing tribe of grandbabies. You are my legacy and my greatest joy. And to the One who's carried us through it all, Jesus, this is for Your glory. Everything good in my life has come from Your hand.

Family, faith, and a whole lotta grit—that's what built this.

Dendy's 10-Step Transition Process
Your Roadmap from being robbed to Keeping The Cash

Step 1: **Run Your Numbers**
Use the Compensation Calculator to compare your actual retail net income

against   the 2.75% model and calculate your annual gap.

Step 2: **Have the Kitchen Table Conversation**
Share the numbers with your spouse, partner, or wise counsel and get full family

support before taking any action.

Step 3: **Consult an Employment Attorney (if necessary)**
Review your non-compete, non-solicitation, and all employment agreements to

know exactly what is enforceable.

Step 4: **Connect With Me** To Talk To Edge Home Finance
Have a transparent conversation with leadership, see the technology, and review

real commission statements.

Step 5: **Talk to Loan Officers Who Have Made the Move**
Hear the real transition experience from loan officers who came from your type

of company.

Step 6: **Secure Your Personal Relationships**
Ensure personal contact information for referral partners and past clients is

stored on your personal devices.

Step 7: **Build Your Financial Bridge**
Set aside 60 to 90 days of living expenses so you transition from a position of

strength, not anxiety.

Step 8: **Submit Your Paperwork and Transfer Your License**
Complete the Edge onboarding package and initiate your license transfer, which

takes 7 to 14 business days.

Step 9: **Give Notice with Grace**
Resign professionally with a brief meeting and a short letter, then prepare for the

predictable phone call.

Step 10: **Launch Your Business and Keep the Cash**
Go live, reconnect with your Realtors, close your first loans, and see 2.75% on a

transparent commission statement.

About Michael Dendy

Michael and Melissa grew up in Marietta, Georgia. As high school sweethearts, they have been married for 33 years. Michael and his wife have 12 kids, 2 daughters-in-law, 1 son-in-law, 2 grand-babies, a dog named Kylo and a turtle named Tot.

After closing hundreds of transactions and seeing the need for a consumer advocate in the real estate and mortgage industry, Michael decided to write this book to expose the industry insider secrets for all consumers.

Michael and Melissa have worked hard to provide key insights that will help their kids navigate through some of life's toughest challenges and biggest decisions. He now compiled a tool that is the same information that he would share with his own kids and wants to help homebuyers realize the dream of homeownership.

"I HAVE 12 KIDS...I CLOSE LOANS!"

Follow on social media, check out michaeldendy.com or email at michael@dendyteam.com

You can reach Michael Dendy by calling him directly at 615-499-6335.

A Note To The Reader

When I published *Homebuying Made Easy for Veterans* in 2019, I was inspired by the stories of service members who had sacrificed so much and deserved a smooth, rewarding path to homeownership. Writing that book taught me the importance of simplifying what can feel like an overwhelming process. It also reminded me that no matter where you start, the journey to owning a home is one of the most transformative experiences in life.

Now, I have also written Homebuying Secrets for Veterans, Homebuying Secrets for First-Time Homebuyers and Homebuying Secrets for the Self-Employed and UNLOCKED: The $847 Billion Theft Hiding In Your Mortgage. All dedicated to the same concept of making the homebuying process easier and educating homebuyers.

As I write this book for exposing the industry and making sure loan officers understand the importance of transparency, My passion for helping other loan officers that are in the same situation that I was in hasn't changed. It's grown! I've seen firsthand how daunting the process can be, from budgeting to being scared, to the "I don't know what I don't know and how the mortgage companies intentionally hides the secrets. That's why I wanted to create a resource that not only demystifies the compensation but also inspires confidence and allows loan officers to become "THE CEO LOAN OFFICER".

Of course, I bring a unique perspective to the table. If you've heard my slogan, you know: *"I HAVE 12 KIDS... I HAVE TO CLOSE LOANS!"* That's more than just a catchphrase; it's a testament to my drive and dedication. With a full house of personalities, dreams, and future homeowners under one roof, I've learned the value of hard work, resilience, and keeping things simple.

This book is not just a guide. This book is a conversation. It is a conversation with you, the loan officer. It's the advice I would give my own kids if they were navigating a company change and how I would help them not get "ripped off" by the mortgage industry.

Let's get started!
Michael Dendy
615-499-6335

THIS PAGE IS INTENTIONALLY LEFT BLANK.

I'VE ALWAYS WANTED TO BE ABLE TO SAY THAT.

I'VE ALWAYS WANTED TO LET CONSUMERS KNOW THAT THIS IS SUCH A WASTE OF PAPER, JUST LIKE THE PAGE THAT IS LEFT BLANK ON YOUR BANK STATEMENT.

IT'S STUPID!

INTRODUCTION

The Day I Realized I Was Already the Boss

Let me tell you about a Wednesday afternoon in Franklin, Tennessee, that rewired the way I think about this business. I was sitting in the parking lot of a Chick-fil-A, engine running, eating a chicken sandwich between appointments, and I had my phone propped up on the steering wheel with my pipeline spreadsheet glowing back at me. I had fourteen loans in various stages of processing. I had just spent my lunch hour at a table with two Realtors who between them were going to send me six or seven purchase deals over the next quarter. Before that I had spent the morning putting out fires on a VA loan that underwriting had kicked back with conditions that made no sense, and I had talked the appraiser into a rush turnaround on a refi that was about to blow its lock expiration. My afternoon was booked with two new applications, a pre-approval call with a first-time buyer who had about forty questions, and a follow-up with a title company that was dragging its feet on a closing package.

I looked at that pipeline spreadsheet and I looked at my calendar and I had a thought that stopped me mid-bite. Who exactly is managing me right now?

Nobody. Not a single person on the planet was telling me what to do that day. My branch manager was not in the car with me. Nobody from corporate had called to check on my schedule. No regional VP had sent me a task list or reviewed my lunch plans or approved the order in which I was returning phone calls. I had generated every single lead in that pipeline through my own relationships. I had structured every deal based on my own product knowledge. I had solved every problem using my own experience and my own judgment. I was running a financial services operation out of the front seat of my jeep, and I was doing it entirely on my own initiative.

And that is when the real question hit me. If I am doing all the work of a business owner, why in the world am I getting paid like an employee?

That question is the reason this book exists. Not the math, although the math will make you angry enough to do something about it. Not the charts, although the charts will show you in black and white exactly how much money is walking out of your life every year. The reason this booklet exists is that one question, and the fact that most loan officers have never stopped long enough between appointments to ask it.

I spent years in this industry before I asked it myself, and I am not a slow learner. I started in Ann Arbor, Michigan, at a retail mortgage bank that paid me 100 basis points per loan. One percent. That sounded fair to me at the time because I had nothing to compare it to and the company made sure I never saw the full revenue picture on any deal I closed. I worked my way up to branch manager and got a "so-called" raise to 125 basis points, which felt like winning the lottery even though it was a quarter of one percent. I moved my family, all twelve kids and my wife Bo, over 700 miles to Franklin for a joint venture position that paid me 80 basis points on the deals that were supposed to be the whole reason for the move. I went broker and saw the light for the first time when my split gave me sixty percent of the total commission and I could finally see what a loan actually generated in revenue. And then I watched that broker shop pick up a correspondent warehouse line and slide right back into the same opacity I thought I had escaped.

Every single one of those stops taught me something, but the lesson that mattered most did not come from a comp plan or a rate sheet. It came from paying attention to what I was actually doing every day and finally admitting to myself that the work I was performing was not the work of someone who punches a clock and waits for instructions. I was acquiring clients. I was managing complex financial transactions. I was building strategic partnerships. I was marketing, consulting, problem-solving, negotiating, and generating every dollar of revenue that my company reported on its books. I was running a business. I just was not getting paid like it.

This book is built around that realization and everything that flows from it. It is not a recruiting pitch and it is not a business plan. It is a mirror. I am going to hold it up and show you what your workday actually looks like when you strip away the titles and the org charts and the language that the retail mortgage industry uses to keep you thinking small. You are going to see a CEO staring back at you, because that is what you are. You are the person who generates the revenue. You are the person who builds the relationships. You are the person who carries the risk, makes the decisions, and loses sleep when a deal is sideways. The company provides a logo and a desk. You provide everything else.

Once you see that clearly, we are going to talk about what it costs you. Not in abstract terms or hypothetical scenarios, but with real numbers based on real production. I am going to show you that the average loan officer producing $18 million a year generates somewhere between $490,000 and $756,000 in total revenue for their company and takes home $150,000 to $165,000 of it. That means you are keeping somewhere between twenty-two and thirty percent of the wealth you create. A CEO who ran any other kind of business on those margins would fire their business model before lunch.

Then we are going to talk about what happens when you stop accepting the employee label and start operating with the CEO mindset. Not a different job. Not different skills. Not different hours. The same you, doing the same work, for the same borrowers and the same Realtors, but inside an economic structure that lets you keep what you earn instead of handing most of it up a management pyramid that does not close a single loan.

I am going to walk you through the three lies the industry uses to keep you from making the shift. I am going to show you a side-by-side P&L that compares your retail income to your income as a CEO Loan Officer in a true broker model, and the difference is not ten percent or twenty percent. It is a quarter of a million dollars a year, every year, for the rest of your career. I am going to give you five pillars for building the operating system that supports a CEO-level business. And I am going to introduce you to a couple named Derek and Karen who sat at their own kitchen table one Tuesday night, ran these same numbers, and discovered they were leaving $595,000 a year on the table between the two of them.

I have twelve kids. That is not a punchline. That is the reason I could not afford to keep pretending that a hundred basis points was a fair deal. When you have that many futures depending on the decisions you make today, you do not have the luxury of comfortable ignorance. Every dollar you leave inside a system that was designed to keep it away from you is a dollar your family will never see. Every year you spend performing CEO-level work for employee-level pay is a year of wealth that does not come back.

Bo and I have been married for thirty-three years. High school sweethearts from Marietta, Georgia, who built a life together one decision at a time. She was with me through every move, every comp plan, every late-night kitchen table conversation about whether the next step was the right one. And the one thing she said to me that I will never forget, the thing that finally pushed me to stop accepting less than I was worth, was five words. "You deserve better than this." She was right. And so do you.

This booklet is the conversation I wish someone had with me fifteen years ago. It would have saved me and my family millions of dollars. I cannot give you those years back, but I can make sure you do not lose another one. The CEO Loan Officer is not a title you earn someday. It is who you already are. The only question left is whether you are going to keep getting paid like one of the employees, or whether you are going to step into the role you have been filling all along and finally collect what you are worth.

Let us get to work.

THE CEO
LOAN OFFICER

You Are Already Running a Business.
It Is Time to Get Paid Like It.

By Michael Dendy
The Mortgage Evangelist

From the book KEEP THE CASH
keepthecash.com

"As long as you are alive, you will either live
to accomplish your own goals and dreams or
be used as a resource to accomplish someone
else's."

- Grant Cardone, The 10X Rule

A Question That Changes Everything

I want you to think about what you did last Tuesday. Not the big moments. The small, ordinary ones that fill an ordinary workday. You woke up, checked your phone, and started responding to borrowers and Realtors before your coffee was cool enough to drink. You followed up on pre-approvals. You checked loan statuses in underwriting. You called a title company about a closing that was drifting sideways. You had lunch with a Realtor and talked about market conditions, rate trends, and which neighborhoods are moving. After lunch you took two new applications, ran credit, and priced three different loan scenarios for a borrower who wanted to see every option laid out side by side. You spent forty-five minutes on the phone with a nervous first-time buyer who had questions about closing costs. You responded to sixteen emails. You updated your pipeline. And somewhere around six or seven in the evening, you finally put the phone down.

Now look at that day and ask yourself one honest question. What part of it was the work of an employee?

None of it. Every single task you performed was the work of a business owner. You generated your own leads through relationships you built with your own sweat and your own reputation. You managed your own pipeline. You consulted with clients on complex financial products. You marketed yourself over lunch. You negotiated timelines with vendors. You problem-solved on the fly when underwriting came back with conditions nobody expected. You managed your own time, set your own priorities, and made dozens of independent decisions that directly affected your income.

There was no manager standing over your shoulder telling you which calls to make. You ran your day the way a CEO runs a company, **because that is exactly what you are.** You are a CEO who has been misclassified as an employee, and that misclassification is costing you a fortune.

The CEO Job Description You Already Fulfill

If I sat down and wrote a formal job description for the CEO of a small financial services company, it would read almost word for word like a description of what you already do every day. The CEO is responsible for client acquisition through personal networking and relationship development. The CEO manages a pipeline of complex financial transactions from origination through closing. The CEO provides expert consultation to clients on a range of financial products and regulatory requirements. The CEO develops and maintains strategic partnerships with real estate professionals, financial planners, attorneys, and other referral sources. The CEO manages vendor relationships with title companies, appraisers, insurance providers, and settlement agents. The CEO is responsible for marketing, branding, and business development. The CEO ensures regulatory compliance across all transactions. And the CEO is accountable for all revenue generation.

Read that paragraph one more time, slowly. Every single function described in it is something you already do. Not some of them. All of them. You are the CEO, the sales team, the marketing department, the client services manager, the compliance officer, and the business development director all rolled into one person. The only thing you are not doing is collecting the revenue that a CEO of a business that size would collect, because your company has structured the arrangement so they keep the majority and hand you back a fraction with a label that says compensation.

CEO Function	What a CEO Does	What YOU Already Do
Sales and Revenue	Generates all company revenue through client relationships	Generate 100% of your production through your own relationships
Marketing	Builds brand, creates awareness, attracts new clients	Attend open houses, host events, build Realtor networks, run social media
Client Services	Manages client experience from first contact to delivery	Guide borrowers from pre-qual through closing, handle every question
Partnerships	Develops strategic alliances with complementary businesses	Build referral networks with Realtors, builders, financial planners, attorneys
Vendor Management	Negotiates and manages third-party service providers	Coordinate with title companies, appraisers, insurance agents, inspectors
Compliance	Ensures all operations meet regulatory standards	Maintain licensing, follow TRID, RESPA, ECOA, and state regulations on every deal
Pipeline Management	Manages workflow, production schedules, delivery timelines	Track every loan from application to closing, manage conditions, meet deadlines

| Financial Consulting | Provides expert guidance on complex financial decisions | Advise borrowers on loan programs, rate structures, down payment strategies |

A CEO running a financial services company that generates $490,000 in annual revenue would expect to take home $300,000 to $400,000 or more. You run that exact business. You take home $150,000 to $180,000.

3 LIES THAT KEEP YOU THINKING LIKE AN EMPLOYEE

The Three Lies That Keep You Thinking Like an Employee

The retail mortgage industry has spent decades perfecting three specific lies that prevent loan officers from seeing themselves as business owners. These lies are woven into the culture, the language, and the compensation structure of every retail bank in the country, and they are so deeply embedded that most loan officers accept them without ever questioning a single word.

Lie Number One: You Need the Company's Infrastructure

This is the foundational lie, and the company invests the most energy in maintaining it. The message is simple: you could never do this on your own because you do not have access to underwriting, processing, compliance, technology, and investor relationships. Without us, you would be lost. The lie works because it contains a grain of truth. You do need infrastructure. You need an LOS, a CRM, a pricing engine, compliance support, and investor relationships. What the company does not want you to know is that every single piece of that infrastructure is available on the open market at a fraction of what they charge you. In a true broker model, you access all of it through third-party vendors who compete for your business. You are not choosing between the company's infrastructure and nothing. You are choosing between their overpriced, proprietary systems and a marketplace of competitive alternatives that cost less and often perform better.

Lie Number Two: Your Income Will Go Down If You Leave

This is the lie your manager tells you when you start asking questions about where the money goes. The pitch sounds something like this: sure, brokers have higher splits, but they also have higher expenses, and when you factor in all the costs of running your own business, you end up making about the same or maybe even less. This is mathematically false. The typical retail loan officer producing $18 million in annual volume earns $150,000 to $180,000 after all deductions. The same loan officer in a true broker model using transparent compensation at 2.75% earns $415,000 to $443,000 on the same volume after paying for all technology, marketing, and overhead at market rates. The income does not go down. It doubles. In many cases it nearly triples. The company knows this, which is exactly why they work so hard to make sure you never see the comparison.

Lie Number Three: Being a Broker Is Risky and Unstable

This is the fear lie, and it is the most insidious of the three because it targets your family. The company wants you to picture yourself alone in a home office with no safety net, no health insurance, no retirement plan, and no guaranteed income. But here is what they hope you never think about long enough to realize. You are already one hundred percent commission. Your company does not pay you a salary. If you do not close loans, you do not earn money. That is already the risk profile of a business owner. The only difference is that a business owner gets to keep the revenue. You carry all the risk of an entrepreneur and receive the compensation of an employee. That is not stability. That is the illusion of stability, and the company charges you between $100,000 and $200,000 a year for that illusion.

The Mindset Shift: Employee vs. CEO Loan Officer

How you think about your business determines how you get paid. Read the left column out loud and then read the right column out loud. Listen to the difference. The left column sounds like someone who has accepted the rules of a game they did not design. The right column sounds like someone who has realized they are the game.

Area	Employee Mindset	CEO Mindset
Compensation	"My comp plan is 100 bps"	"I generate $490K in revenue. What percentage do I keep?"
Technology	"The company provides my tools"	"What do these tools cost, and can I buy them for less?"
Marketing	"The company handles marketing"	"Whose brand are they building with my relationships?"
Client Data	"My contacts are in the CRM"	"Who owns that data when I leave?"
Risk	"At least I have a stable job"	"I am 100% commission. I already carry all the risk."
Fees	"Those are just the cost of doing business"	"Every hidden fee is money I earned and someone else took"

| Career Path | "Maybe I will get promoted to manager" | "I already run this business. I just need to own it." |
| Non-Compete | "I cannot leave because of my agreement" | "A piece of paper is not worth $200K a year of my family's future" |

The shift from the left column to the right column is not a career change. It is a perspective change. And perspective is the most valuable thing you can own in this industry, because the moment you see yourself as the CEO of your own financial services company, every decision you make from that point forward changes.

The Revenue You Actually Generate

Let me put real numbers on the CEO Loan Officer concept, because this section needs to land with the force of a sledgehammer. These numbers are based on an average producing loan officer at $18 million in annual volume, closing approximately 48 loans per year at an average loan amount of $375,000.

The total revenue generated on a single loan includes origination income, lender premium or yield spread, processing and administrative fees, and servicing rights value. On a $375,000 loan, that total ranges from $10,200 to $15,750 depending on the company's rate sheet structure and investor relationships. Using a conservative midpoint of $10,200 per loan, your 48 annual loans generate $489,600 in total revenue for the company. Using the higher end, you generate $756,000. Either way, you are responsible for creating roughly half a million to three quarters of a million dollars in annual revenue.

Your take-home compensation on 48 loans at 100 basis points on $375,000 per loan is $180,000 before any deductions. After technology fees, CRM charges, marketing allocations, E&O deductions, and per-loan fees, your net take-home is typically $150,000 to $165,000. That means you are keeping somewhere between twenty-two and thirty-four percent of the total revenue you generate. The company keeps the rest.

Revenue Line Item	Conservative	High End
LO Origination Income (100 bps x 48 loans)	$180,000	$180,000
Lender Premium / Yield Spread	$139,200	$315,600
Processing and Admin Fees	$50,400	$81,600
Servicing Rights Value	$120,000	$178,800
TOTAL REVENUE YOU GENERATE	$489,600	$756,000
Your Net Take-Home After Deductions	$150,000	$165,000
COMPANY RETAINS	$339,600	$591,000
YOUR SHARE OF REVENUE YOU CREATED	30.6%	21.8%

You keep between 21.8% and 30.6% of the revenue you create. The company keeps the rest. Nobody would agree to those terms if they were stated that clearly.

Your P&L as a CEO Loan Officer

If you took the same $18 million in production and ran it through a true broker model at 2.75% transparent compensation, the revenue picture changes so dramatically it will make you rethink every year you have spent in retail. The math is straightforward. On $18 million at 2.75%, your gross compensation is $495,000. Now subtract every legitimate business expense you would carry as an independent broker operating at market rates.

Your LOS license costs $75 per month, or $900 a year. Your CRM runs $100 per month, or $1,200 a year. Your pricing engine costs $50 per month, or $600 a year. Marketing, which you control entirely and direct toward building your own brand instead of someone else's logo, runs $500 per month, or $6,000 a year. Compliance and licensing costs run about $3,600 per year. E&O insurance is $1,200 a year. Processing support, whether you hire a processor or use a service, runs $500 to $750 per loan, or $24,000 to $36,000 per year. Office overhead averages $6,000 to $12,000 a year. Health insurance for a family plan runs $8,400 to $18,000 a year depending on your state and coverage.

Add every one of those expenses together and your total operating costs as a CEO Loan Officer range from $51,900 to $79,500 per year. Subtract that from your $495,000 gross compensation and your net income is $415,500 to $443,100.

Line Item	Retail Employee	CEO Broker
Gross Compensation	$180,000	$495,000
Technology (LOS, CRM, Pricing)	(Deducted already)	($2,700)
Marketing (YOUR brand, YOUR tools)	(Deducted already)	($6,000)
Processing Costs ($500-$750/loan)	(Deducted already)	($24,000-$36,000)
Compliance, Licensing, E&O	(Deducted already)	($4,800)
Office Overhead	(Deducted already)	($6,000-$12,000)
Health Insurance (family plan)	(Not provided)	($8,400-$18,000)
Retail Hidden Deductions	($15,000-$30,000)	$0
NET ANNUAL INCOME	$150,000-$165,000	$415,500-$443,100
10-YEAR CAREER EARNINGS	$1.5M-$1.65M	$4.15M-$4.43M

Same loan officer. Same volume. Same borrowers. Same Realtors. Same work ethic. The only thing that changes is the economic structure around you. The gap is $250,000 to $293,000 per year.

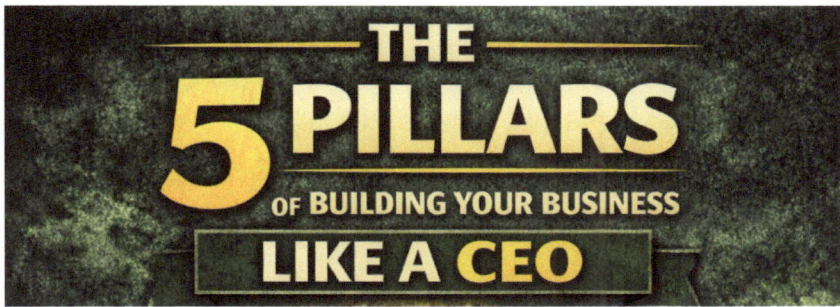
THE
5 PILLARS
OF BUILDING YOUR BUSINESS
LIKE A CEO

Building Your CEO Operating System

Seeing yourself as the CEO is the first step. Building the system that supports that identity is what turns the mindset into money. Every successful CEO operates on a framework of repeatable systems, not random bursts of effort. The loan officers who thrive after making the transition are the ones who build their business on five core pillars, each one reinforcing the others.

Pillar 1: Own Your Relationships

Your Realtor relationships, your past client database, and your professional network are the most valuable assets in your business. In retail, those relationships live on a company server that you lose access to the day you walk out the door. The CEO Loan Officer stores every contact, every referral partner phone number, every past client email address on personal devices and personal systems that belong to you. Not the company. You. Start today. Export your contacts to a personal spreadsheet, a personal CRM, or even a handwritten notebook that you keep at home. Every relationship you have built with your own effort belongs to you, and you need to make sure the record of that relationship is in your possession before anything else changes.

Pillar 2: Own Your Brand

In retail, every marketing dollar you spend or that gets deducted from your paycheck builds the company's brand. Their logo on the flyer. Their name on the pre-approval letter. Their website on the business card. When you leave, all of that brand equity stays behind and benefits the next loan officer who sits in your chair. The CEO Loan Officer invests in their own brand from day one. Your name. Your face. Your story. Your reputation. Build a personal website. Create social media content under your own identity. Develop a referral partner presentation that features you, not a corporate logo. Every dollar you invest in your personal brand compounds over your entire career because it travels with you wherever you go.

Pillar 3: Own Your Technology Stack

The retail model charges you $200 to $400 a month for technology that costs $50 to $100 on the open market. More importantly, when you use company-provided technology, you are building workflows and storing data inside systems you do not control. The CEO Loan Officer selects and pays for their own tools at market rates. Your LOS subscription. Your CRM account. Your pricing portal. Your document storage. When you own your tech stack, you control your data, you control your workflow, and you never have to start over from scratch because a company changed platforms or because you changed companies.

Pillar 4: Own Your Process

The most successful CEO Loan Officers have a documented, repeatable process for every stage of the loan cycle. A step-by-step onboarding sequence for new borrowers. A weekly touchpoint schedule for active pipeline files. A closing follow-up system that turns every closed loan into a future referral. A quarterly outreach calendar for Realtors and referral partners. When your process is documented and repeatable, your business runs on systems instead of memory. You can train an assistant to follow the system. You can scale without working more hours. And you can take a vacation without your pipeline falling apart, because the system keeps running whether you are sitting at your desk or sitting on a beach.

Pillar 5: Own Your Numbers

The CEO of any company knows their numbers cold. Revenue per unit. Cost of acquisition. Profit margin per transaction. Operating expenses as a percentage of gross income. The CEO Loan Officer tracks these same metrics for their mortgage business. How much revenue does each loan generate? What is your average commission per closing? What does your marketing cost per lead? What is your conversion rate from application to closing? What is your net income after all expenses? When you know your numbers, you make decisions based on data instead of emotion. You stop accepting compensation structures that sound good in a recruiting pitch and start evaluating them against the actual economics of your production. The numbers do not lie, and the numbers are the CEO Loan Officer's most powerful weapon against the industry's carefully constructed illusions.

A Kitchen Table That Changed Everything

I want to tell you about a couple named Derek and Karen who both worked as loan officers at the same retail bank in Nashville. They were married to each other and between the two of them they produced about $34 million per year. Combined retail income sat right around $340,000. Good money by any standard, and they were grateful for it. They had four kids, a nice house in Franklin, and a life that looked comfortable from the outside.

Derek read an early draft of this material. He did the math on a Tuesday night after the kids were in bed, using the same formulas you have seen in these pages. When Karen came downstairs and found him at the kitchen table with a calculator and a legal pad, she asked what he was working on. He turned the legal pad around so she could read it. At the top he had written their combined retail income: $340,000. Below that, he had calculated their combined income in a true broker model at 2.75%: $935,000. Below that, he had written a single sentence: "We are leaving $595,000 on the table every year."

Karen sat down. They talked until two in the morning. They ran the numbers again. They calculated their expenses. They called an employment attorney the next day about their non-competes. Three months later, they moved their licenses. Their first full year as independent brokers, their combined income was $867,000. Not quite the $935,000 on the legal pad, because they were still building some of their systems. But $867,000 is a long way from $340,000.

Derek told me the only thing he regrets is not doing it five years earlier, because that delay cost them nearly $3 million.

The CEO Daily Operating Framework

The difference between a loan officer who earns $150,000 and a CEO Loan Officer who earns $400,000 or more is not talent. It is not connections. It is not luck. It is how they structure their day. Below is a framework that treats every hour of your workday like the valuable asset it is. This is not a rigid schedule. It is a philosophy of intentional time allocation that ensures the highest-value activities in your business never get crowded out by the urgent but low-value tasks that consume most loan officers' days.

Time Block	CEO Activity	Why It Matters
7:00 - 8:00 AM	Pipeline review, underwriting follow-up, condition clearing	Protect your closings. Revenue in the pipeline is revenue earned.
8:00 - 10:00 AM	Outbound relationship calls: Realtors, past clients, referral partners	Revenue generation. This is the CEO's highest-value activity.
10:00 - 12:00 PM	New applications, pre-approvals, pricing scenarios, client consultations	Serve the clients your morning calls produced. Convert interest into pipeline.
12:00 - 1:00 PM	Relationship lunch with a Realtor or referral partner	One relationship lunch per week produces 10-15 additional referrals per year.
1:00 - 3:00 PM	File management, processor coordination, document collection	Operational execution. Keep the machine running so closings stay on schedule.
3:00 - 4:00 PM	Marketing and brand building: social content, email outreach, personal website	Invest in the asset that travels with you. Your brand compounds over time.
4:00 - 5:00 PM	Numbers review: daily production, weekly pipeline, monthly P&L tracking	The CEO who knows the numbers makes better decisions than the one who guesses.

Your First Five Steps

You do not need to become a different person to make this shift. You do not need to learn new skills, change your work habits, or reinvent your career. You need to see yourself clearly, and then you need to act on what you see. Here are the first five steps that take you from reading about the CEO Loan Officer to becoming one.

Step 1: Run Your Numbers

Go to keepthecash.com and use the Compensation Calculator. Plug in your actual production volume, your current comp rate, and your real take-home after all deductions. Then compare it to the 2.75% transparent model. Write the gap on a piece of paper and tape it to your bathroom mirror where you will see it every morning. That number is what you are leaving on the table this year.

Step 2: Have the Kitchen Table Conversation

Sit down with your spouse, your partner, or your most trusted advisor and share what you have learned. Show them the numbers. Talk about the timeline. Discuss the financial bridge you will need for the transition. This decision affects your whole family, and the people who love you deserve to be part of it from the beginning.

Step 3: Ask the Seven Questions

Walk into your manager's office and ask the seven questions outlined in Keep The Cash, Chapter 7. Ask about total loan revenue. Ask about your effective take-home after all deductions. Ask who owns your client data. Ask how many people get paid when you close a loan. Pay close attention to the answers you get, and pay even closer attention to the questions they refuse to answer.

Step 4: Talk to Someone Who Has Made the Move

Find a loan officer who has transitioned from retail to the true broker model and ask them to tell you the truth about their experience. What surprised them? What was harder than expected? What was easier? And most importantly, what does their commission statement look like compared to what they made in retail?

Step 5: Connect with Edge Home Finance

Call me directly at 615-499-6335 or visit keepthecash.com. Have a transparent conversation with leadership, see the technology platform, and review real commission statements from real loan officers. No pressure. No pitch. Just the truth and the math.

You built the relationships.

You earned the referrals.

You closed the loans.

Now keep the cash.

Michael Dendy | The Mortgage Evangelist
615-499-6335
keepthecash.com

From the book KEEP THE CASH by Michael Dendy

FINAL WORD

Look, I've spent the last 100+ pages showing you how the mortgage industry works, where the money goes, and how to protect yourself. But here's what matters most: you now have a choice. You can walk into the future of your career armed with knowledge, or you can go in blind and hope for the best. Hope is not a strategy, and the industry is counting on you to stay confused.

Do your research. Ask the hard questions. Call me, someone who welcomes transparency instead of hiding behind industry jargon and "proprietary information" excuses. The smoke and mirrors act that the industry teaches only works on people who don't know the tricks. You know them now. Use that knowledge. Edge Home Finance will respect you more for asking tough questions, not less. And if they don't respect you for being informed, they don't deserve you as a loan officer.

I've got twelve kids, and every single one of them would get this advice before they work in the mortgage industry. I'm not going to let them walk into a career and $MILLIONS because some manager saw an easy mark.

This book is the same advice I'm giving them, and I'm giving it to you for the same reason: because I have a choice.
1-I can go through life and be a "SUCCESS" and win awards, and be the best. That is all about me.
2-I can go through like and be a "SURVIVOR" and talk about everything I have overcome and how it made me better. That is also about me.
3-I can make the choice to be "SIGNIFICANT". This is about YOU. Can I wake up every single day I find a way to give myself to others.

If you want more straight talk about money, careers, parenting, and navigating life's biggest decisions without getting ripped off, follow me at @DadWith12Kids. I'll keep telling you the truth, even when it makes people uncomfortable. That's what dads do.

Now go keep your cash.